I0115819

ANIMAL CREATIONS
COLORING BOOK
FOR ADULTS
RELAXING STRESS RELIEVING DESIGNS

All rights reserved.
No part of this book may be
reproduced in any form without
written permission of the
copyright owners. If you
would like to see more images
and stay updated on new books,
visit

www.facebook.com/AdultColoringBooksSelahWorks
www.selahworks.com

Printed in the U.S.A.
Copyright © 2015 Cindy Elsharouni
All rights reserved.
ISBN:10:0692585419
ISBN-13:9780692585412

FREE COLORING PAGES EVERY MONTH!!!

GO HERE TO GET FREE COLORING PAGES SENT TO YOUR INBOX MONTHLY!

www.freemonthlycoloringpages.pagedemo.co

LOVE HORSES? GET THE FIRST VOLUME
THE AMAZING WORLD OF HORSES

THE
AMAZING WORLD
OF HORSES
ADULT COLORING BOOK

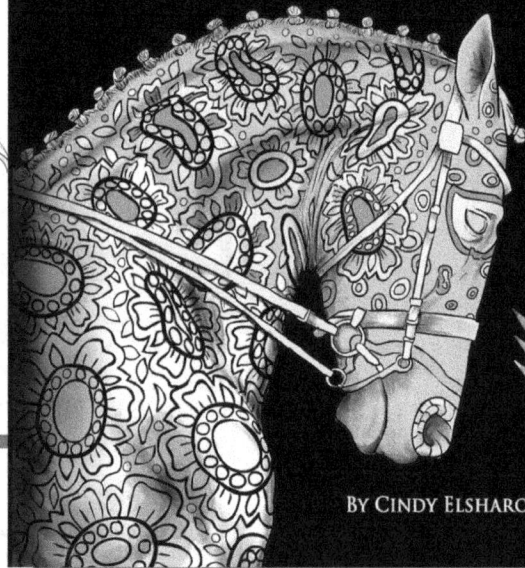

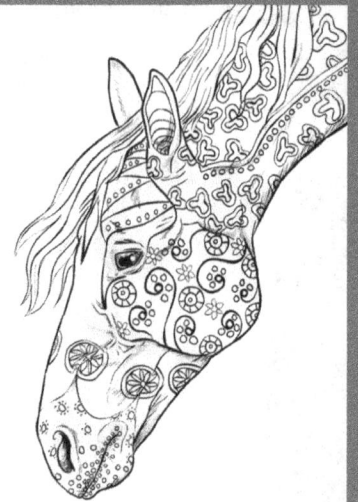

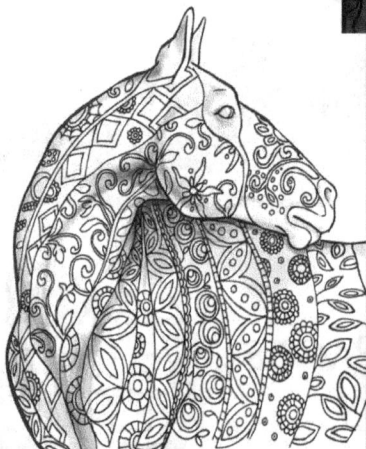

BY CINDY ELSHAROUNI

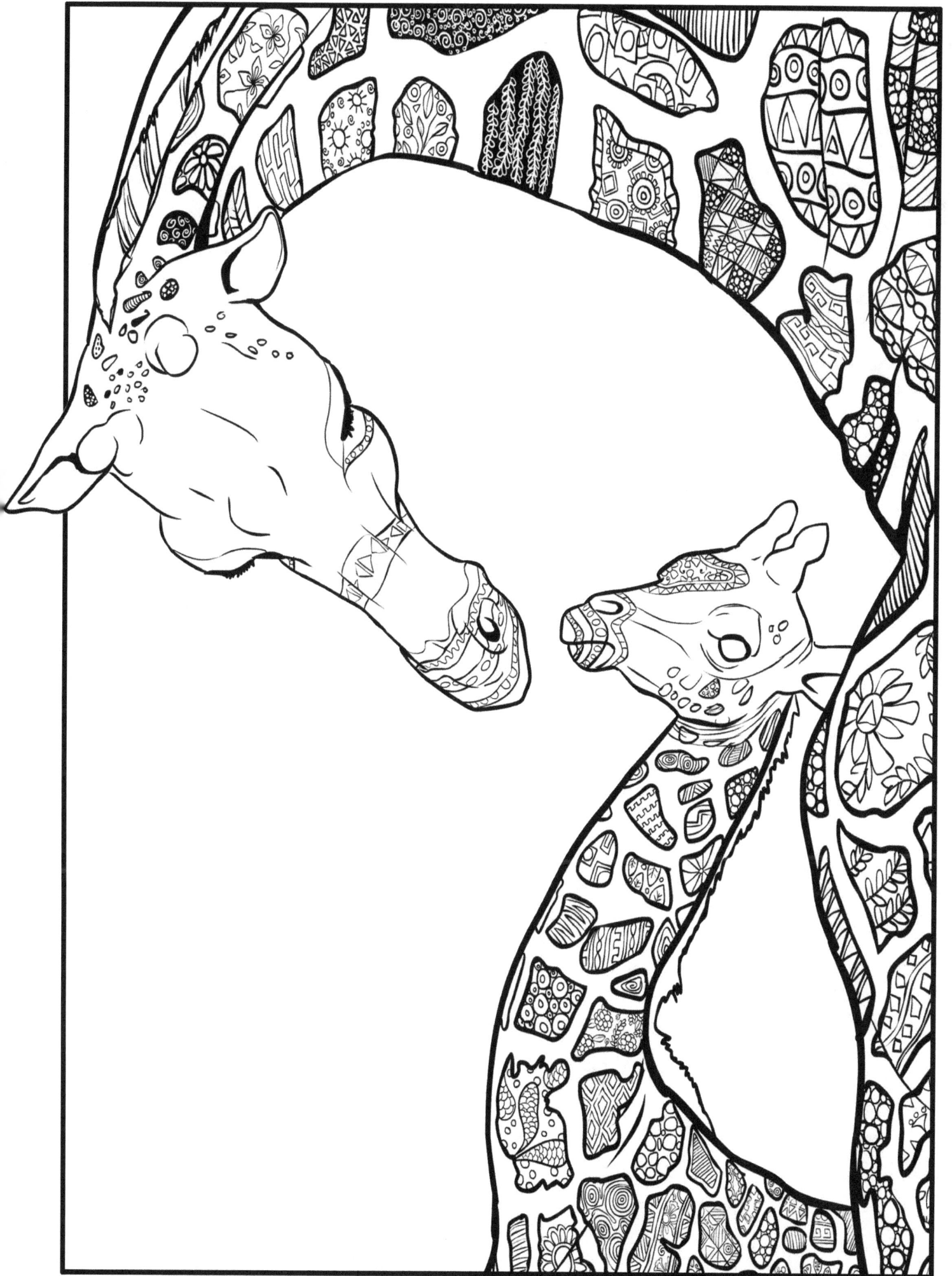

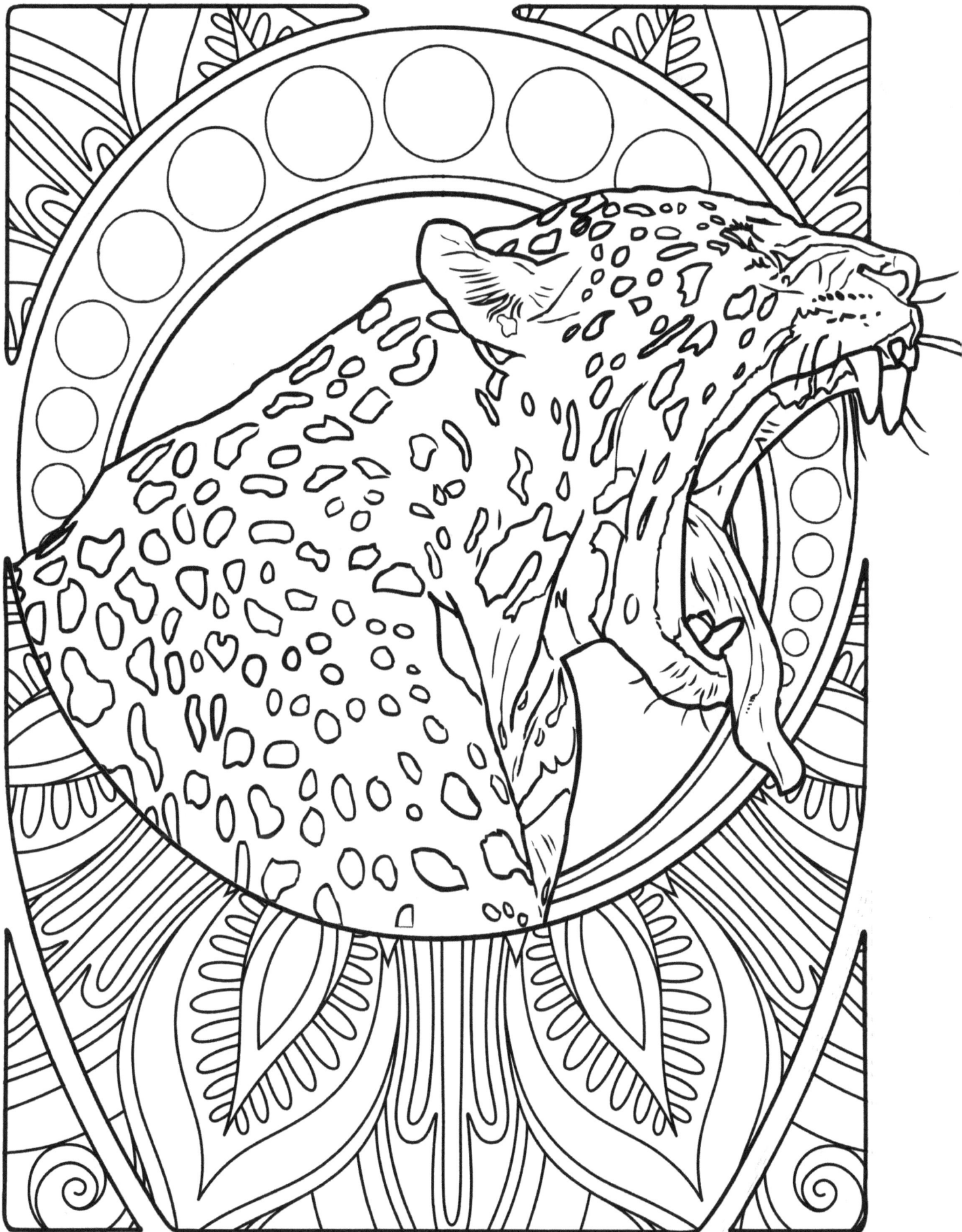

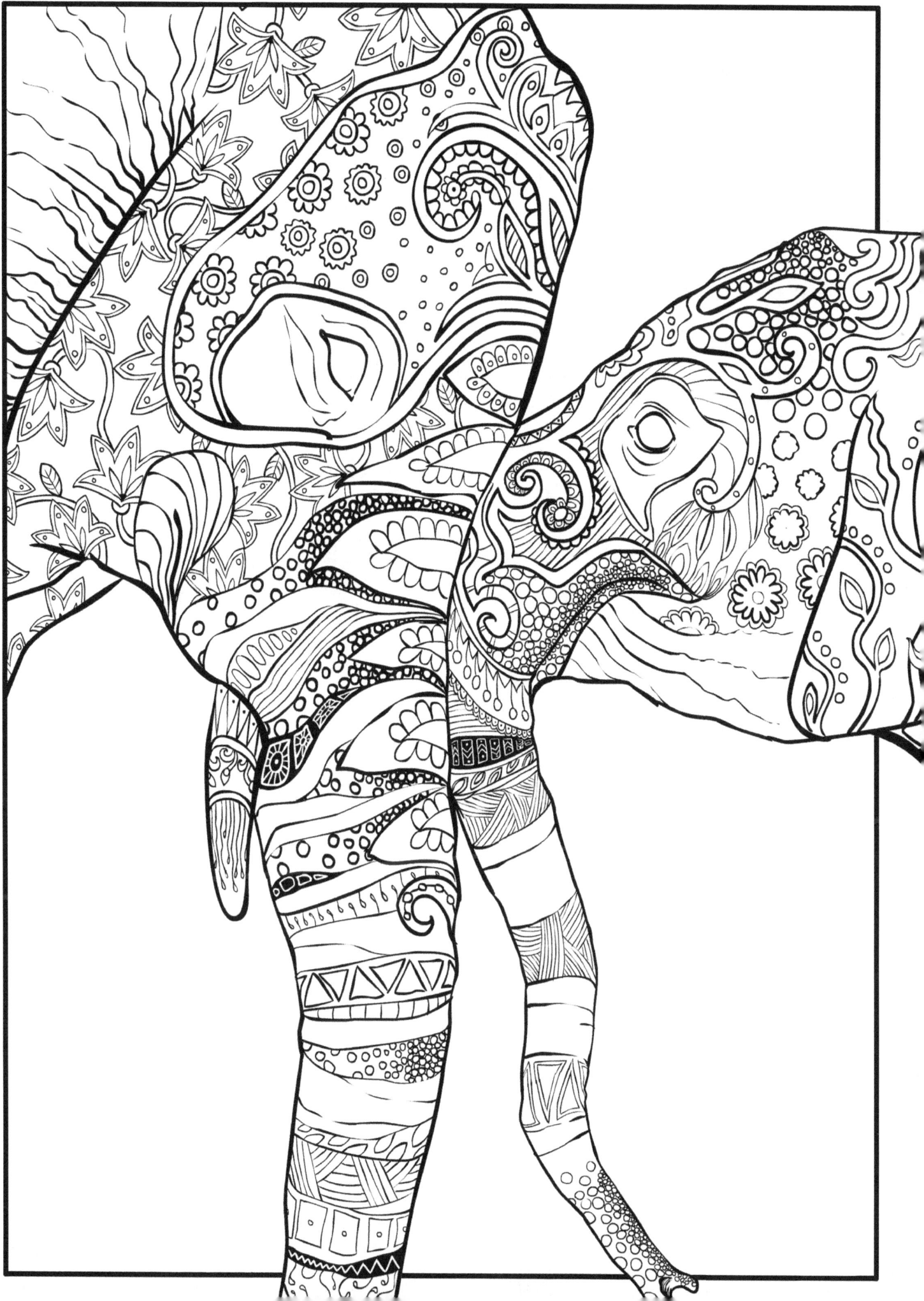

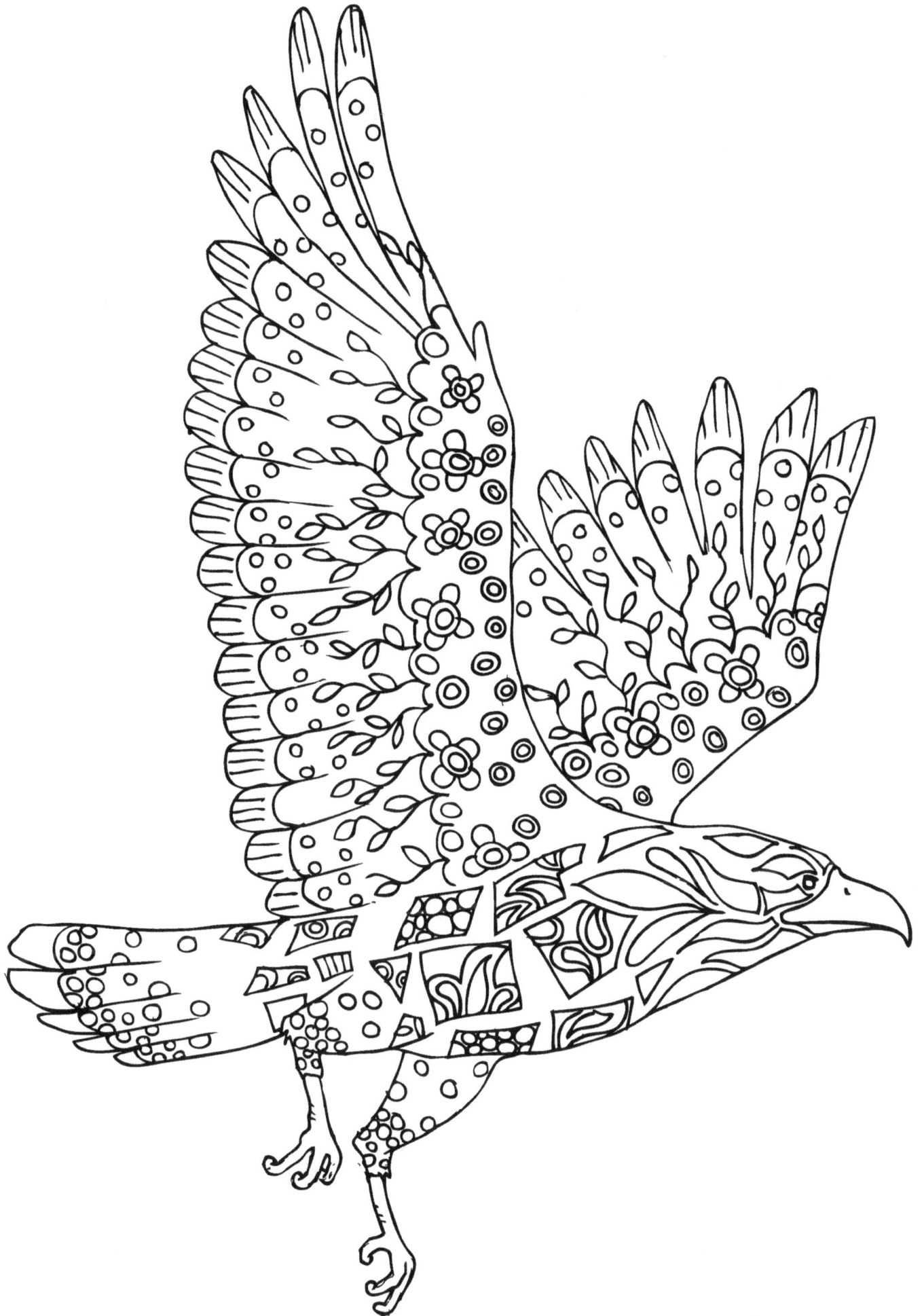

www.ingramcontent.com/pod-product-compliance
Lightning Source LLC
Chambersburg PA
CBHW081649270326
41933CB00018B/3403

* 9 7 8 0 6 9 2 5 8 5 4 1 2 *